FAIRY TALES, FOLKTALES, AND FABLES - LESSON PLANS FOR TEACHERS FOR GRADES K-8

by Steven M. Gregory

Table of Contents

Overview

This set of four lesson plans, designed to take approximately one hour each to complete, explores fairy tales, folktales, and fables. These lessons look at examples of each type of story from different cultures around the world and engage students in the written or oral discussion of the lessons of each story, the story's characteristics, and the differences from one type of story to another.

This set of lesson plans is written in accordance with educational learning standards. They are applicable for grades K-8 with some modifications for grade levels.

Referenced works within these lesson plans are in the public domain and have been provided along with these lesson plans.

What is a Fairy Tale?

Purpose:

This lesson satisfies content standards for multicultural studies and language arts. Students will read (or be read to), discuss, and then produce a written component (optional for lower grades). Students are introduced to fairy tales through two example stories that illustrate the type of tale and the culture it comes from.

Learning outcome(s):

Students will identify the story's lesson or moral, identify characters in the story and their role (protagonist, antagonist, etc.), and discuss cultural aspects of the story. Students will be able to define a fairy tale.

Bridge-in:

As most fairy tales are hundreds or thousands of years old, ask students to imagine what life was like back then. How did people explain things like the weather, earthquakes, or even how the universe came to exist? Student responses should lead them to the idea of supernatural beings. If these supernatural beings existed, where were they? Students may respond that they are everywhere, which can lead into the idea of why can they not be seen? Students should eventually respond that these supernatural beings are in the skies/heavens. If there were supernatural beings in the heavens, what about on the planet with humans? Could the presence of supernatural beings influence what happens to people?

Ask students to think of different fairy tales. Common ones include "Cinderella," "Snow White," and "Sleeping Beauty." Note that tales such as "Peter Rabbit" and "John Henry" are NOT fairy tales. Merriam-Webster provides a good, specific definition of fairy tales as "a story (as for children) involving fantastic forces and beings (such as fairies, wizards, and goblins)."

It's important to note that a story like "Goldilocks and the Three Bears" is often considered a fairy tale, though stricter definitions place it in the folktale category. Fables, such as those by Aesop, also do not qualify as fairy tales.

Another key component to fairy tales is that they are more often stories where the intended audience is children.

Input from you:

Read to students (for older grades, have students read) the two tales, "The Frog Prince" and "Rumpelstiltskin."

Guided Practice:

After the stories, have students write down and/or recall the names of the characters and the tasks that each hero had to overcome. For each tale, ask students:

- Who was the hero?

- Who was the villain?

- What was the magical part of each tale that made it a fairy tale?

- What are the cultural aspects in each tale? That is, what aspects are there to the tale that would make it inappropriate to be told in China or Africa, for example.

For "The Frog Prince," which is French in origin, what does the story tell us about the royal family? Is the king a good king? What about the princess? Does this perception of people "born into royalty" hold true? Remember that the French Revolution was when the people revolted and overthrew the aristocracy because of how they were treated. For "Rumpelstiltskin," which is German in origin, what does it tell us about the interaction between the royal family and commoners? Is there a strong separation? Even though the king makes harsh demands on the miller's daughter he is willing to marry her. What does that tell us about the relationship of German royalty and the people they ruled over? Note that in Germany even today there are members of royal families who are princes, princesses, and barons.

Closure & Assessment:

Ask students to keep in mind that these were fairy tales because of magical elements. Because of these magical elements, fairy tales were most often told to children. Even so, remind students that there are lessons in even these tales that are important. Ask students to keep these facts in mind as they will need to remember them for the next lesson.

What is a Folktale?

<table>
<tr><td>

Purpose:

This lesson satisfies content standards for multicultural studies and language arts. Students will read (or be read to), discuss, and then produce a written component (optional for lower grades). Students are introduced to folktales through two examples that illustrate the type of tale and the culture it comes from.

</td></tr>
<tr><td>

Learning outcome(s):

Students will identify the story's lesson or moral, identify characters in the story and their role (protagonist, antagonist, etc.), and discuss cultural aspects of the story. Students will be able to define a folktale.

</td></tr>
<tr><td>

Bridge-in:

Ask students to imagine what society was like 60 years ago when televisions were not in every household. Then have students go back further to just over 100 years ago before radio was invented. How did people amuse themselves? Students may respond with games or outdoor activities. Guide students into ways people may have amused or entertained themselves at night or during storms so that students come around to stories. When people told stories, were these stories necessarily true? Who listened to these stories? Students should be reminded that extended families often lived together and that grandparents, parents, and children many times shared a home.

</td></tr>
</table>

Pre-test:

Ask students to think of different folktales. Note that tall tales such as "John Henry" and "Paul Bunyan" fall into this category. In addition to tall tales, folktales could include "Peter Rabbit," "Goldilocks and the Three Bears," "Little Red Riding Hood," and "Hansel & Gretel." Folktales may include some supernatural elements, such as talking animals or even people called "witches," but any magic or magic element is not a key part of the story. Folktales are often meant for audiences of all ages. Another key component of folktales is that they are regional and therefore most important to the people from where the tale originated. Folktales incorporate aspects of the region or people where they originated. Folktales are a subset of the overall category of folklore.

Input from you:

Have students read (or read aloud to them) "The Tale of Peter Rabbit" and "Brer Rabbit and the Tar Baby." Note that this is a "retold" version of the Brer Rabbit story, so there are a few details missing but it is much more palatable for younger audiences. The original version of the story can be found online though the dialect can make it difficult to read (https://archive.org/details/uncleremushisson01harr/mode/2up).

Guided Practice:

After the stories, have students write down and/or recall the names of the characters and story plots. For Peter Rabbit:

- Who is the protagonist?
- Who is the antagonist?
- Even though the story is about Peter, is Peter really a good character?
- This is a British story from 1902, so students should understand that there was a great disparity between the aristocracy and the common people. How is this shown in the story?
- Why is Mr. McGregor a bad character?
- How does that reflect the view of common folk toward the ruling class?
- What is the lesson we learn from this story?

For Brer Rabbit, this is a tale from the South in the U.S. during slavery. Brer Rabbit represents the slaves while Brer Fox represents the slave owners. In the original version of the tale, the conflict starts when Brer Fox invites Brer Rabbit to dinner...only Brer Rabbit is supposed to be dinner.

- What does this say about the relationship between slaves and owners? Student responses may include answers relating to how slaves were not seen as equal to slave owners or that slaves were simply an easy means by which slave owners put food on their table.
- Brer Rabbit ends up escaping at the end of the story. How?
- How does this reflect on the "weapons" slaves had to use against their owners in real life?
- What lessons are there to learn from this tale?

Closure & Assessment:

Folktales were so called because they were told by plain "folk," the regular person. Where fairy tales generally were meant for younger audiences, folktales were often told to everyone, including adults. Because folktales often made fun of real people, these real people were turned into characters in the tales that could not be easily identified so that tellers and listeners would not be punished. Even more than fairy tales, folktales taught valuable life lessons. Have students keep this in mind.

What is a Fable?

<table>
<tr><td>

Purpose:

This lesson satisfies content standards for multicultural studies and language arts. Students will read (or be read to), discuss, and then produce a written component (optional for lower grades). Students are introduced to fables through three examples that illustrate the type of tale.

</td></tr>
<tr><td>

Learning outcome(s):

Students will identify the fable's lesson or moral, identify characters in the fable and their role (protagonist, antagonist, etc.), and discuss cultural aspects of the story. Students will be able to define a fable.

</td></tr>
<tr><td>

Bridge-in:

Ask students to imagine what the world and society were like two thousand years ago. There was no running water, no electricity, and most of the people in society could not read or write. How then could people learn the rules for living in their society -- or just getting along with others -- without some means of being taught? What might be the best ways to teach people these societal rules? How could you get someone to pay attention to the lessons? How could you get someone to remember the lessons? Student responses should focus on, or be guided to, the idea that entertaining lessons would be easiest to remember and would get listeners to pay attention to them.

</td></tr>
</table>

Pre-test:

Ask students: What is a fable? Merriam-Webster defines a fable as "a short story that usually is about animals and that is intended to teach a lesson." Ask students to name any fables they might be able to think of. Common answers may be "The Hare and the Tortoise," "The Fox and the Grapes," and "The Ants and the Grasshopper."

Input from you:

Have students read (or read aloud to them) "The Jay and the Peacock," "The Crow and the Pitcher," and "Tale of the Three Fishes." Optionally, for older grades, you can also read "The Lion that Sprang to Life." Additional tales of Aesop can be found here: http://www.aesopfables.com/ Additional tales from the Panchatantra can be found here: http://panchatantra.org/panchatantra-stories.html (Note that not all of the Panchatantra stories are pleasant for young readers/listeners.)

Guided Practice:

Ask students to write down and/or recall the main characters of these fables. Are any of the characters really "bad" characters in these stories? Fables are often very short. Ask students if there is a benefit to a story that is this short. In most fables, especially those by Aesop, the characters are animals. Is there a benefit to the storyteller/listener in hearing stories that feature animals? How might a story that uses animals have broader appeal than one that uses actual people?

Closure & Assessment:

Have students think about the three types of tales that have been discussed: folktales, fairy tales, and fables. Have them consider that all three types provide some form of lesson on how people should live their lives. Because the lessons in fables are often stated or very obvious, they are stories most often remembered as having these life lessons. Even so, note that each type of tale also offers something else. Folktales tend to focus on a specific group of people; fairy tales tend to focus on a specific area or region; fables tend to be universal.

Further Study

Purpose:

This lesson satisfies content standards for multicultural studies and language arts. Students will read (or be read to), discuss, and then produce a written component (optional for lower grades). Students are introduced to fables through three examples that illustrate the type of tale.

Learning outcome(s):

Students will reinforce what they have learned about fairy tales, folktales, and fables. Students will be able to identify each type of tale, identify cultural aspects of a tale, and identify a lesson or moral in the tale.

Input from you:

Have students read (or read aloud to them) "The Frog" (fairy tale), "The Story of the Devotee Who Spilt the Jar of Honey and Oil" (fable), and "The Mirror of Matsuyama" (folktale).

Guided Practice:

Either in writing or orally:

- Ask students to identify the type of each tale.

- What are the aspects of the tale that caused them to choose a category?

    - For the fairy tale, is there a moral or lesson in the story? Students may answer that the lesson is telling the listener to go beyond appearances.

    - Is there anything in the fairy tale that speaks about the relationship of royalty and the people over whom they rule? What does the story say about the prince? Students may answer that royalty did not see a tremendous difference in themselves and the people they ruled. Students may answer that the prince values the traits of the frog more than her appearance.

    - For the fable, which does not include an animal, what is the moral? Note that this is a type of tale categorized as an "air castle" tale in which someone imagines wealth or fame only to have it vanish.

    - For the folktale, have students identify the cultural aspects that make this story appropriate to Japan but perhaps not to Europe or the United States. Students may answer that the daughter's quiet nature would not fit Western world ideals.

    - What lessons does this folktale teach about jumping to conclusions? What lessons does it teach about forgiveness? What about love and devotion?

- In many stories, it is sometimes circumstances that are "bad" and not people. Have students write or discuss if there were "bad" people or "bad" circumstances in these stories.

Additional Ideas:

Teachers may want to engage students in reader's theatre or oral recitation of selected stories. Reader's theater scripts can be found in libraries and online.

For Grades 3 and above, students can be asked to compile a list of lessons, morals, and/or aphorisms then decide what form of tale would best illustrate this. For example, a good deed is often repaid with a good deed might best be illustrated by a fable, e.g., "The Lion and the Mouse." They can then take time to compose and then read or perform the tale. Students in the audience can be asked to determine the type of tale and the lesson.

The Frog Prince

Germany

A translation of the Brothers Grimm's "Frog King" by Edgar Taylor

One fine evening a young princess went into a wood, and sat down by the side of a cool spring of water. She had a golden ball in her hand, which was her favorite plaything, and she amused herself with tossing it into the air and catching it again as it fell. After a time she threw it up so high that when she stretched out her hand to catch it, the ball bounded away and rolled along upon the ground, till at last it fell into the spring. The princess looked into the spring after her ball; but it was very deep, so deep that she could not see the bottom of it.

Then she began to lament her loss, and said, "Alas! If I could only get my ball again, I would give all my fine clothes and jewels, and everything that I have in the world."

Whilst she was speaking a frog put its head out of the water and said, "Princess, why do you weep so bitterly?"

"Alas!" said she, "What can you do for me, you nasty frog? My golden ball has fallen into the spring."

The frog said, "I want not your pearls and jewels and fine clothes; but if you will love me and let me live with you, and eat from your little golden plate, and sleep upon your little bed, I will bring you your ball again."

"What nonsense," thought the princess, "This silly frog is talking! He can never get out of the well. However, he may be able to get my ball for me; and therefore I will promise him what he asks." So she said to the frog, "Well, if you will bring me my ball, I promise to do all you require."

Then the frog put his head down, and dived deep under the water; and after a little while he came up again with the ball in his mouth, and threw it on the ground. As soon as the young princess saw her ball, she ran to pick it up, and was so overjoyed to have it in her hand again, that she never thought of the frog, but ran home with it as fast as she could.

The frog called after her, "Stay, princess, and take me with you as you promised." But she did not stop to hear a word.

The next day, just as the princess had sat down to dinner, she heard a strange noise, tap-tap, as if somebody was coming up the marble staircase. And soon afterwards something knocked gently at the door, and said,

Open the door, my princess dear,

Open the door to thy true love here!

And mind the words that thou and I said

By the fountain cool in the greenwood shade.

Then the princess ran to the door and opened it, and there she saw the frog, whom she had quite forgotten. She was terribly frightened, and shutting the door as fast as she could, came back to her seat. The king, her father, asked her what had frightened her.

"There is a nasty frog," said she, "at the door, who lifted my ball out of the spring this morning. I promised him that he should live with me here, thinking that he could never get out of the spring; but there he is at the door and wants to come in!"

While she was speaking the frog knocked again at the door, and said,

Open the door, my princess dear,

Open the door to thy true love here!

And mind the words that thou and I said

By the fountain cool in the greenwood shade.

The king said to the young princess, "As you have made a promise, you must keep it. So go and let him in."

She did so, and the frog hopped into the room, and came up close to the table. "Pray lift me upon a chair," said he to the princess, "and let me sit next to you." As soon as she had done this, the frog said, "Put your plate closer to me that I may eat out of it." This she did. And when he had eaten as much as he could, he said, "Now I am tired. Carry me upstairs and put me into your little bed."

And the princess took him up in her hand and put him upon the pillow of her own little bed, where he slept all night long. As soon as it was light he jumped up, hopped downstairs, and went out of the house.

"Now," thought the princess, "he is gone, and I shall be troubled with him no more."

But she was mistaken; for when night came again, she heard the same tapping at the door, and when she opened it, the frog came in and slept upon her pillow as before till the morning broke.

And the third night he did the same; but when the princess awoke on the following morning, she was astonished to see, instead of the frog, a handsome prince gazing on her with the most beautiful eyes that ever were seen, and standing at the head of her bed.

He told her that he had been enchanted by a malicious fairy, who had changed him into the form of a frog, in which he was fated to remain till some princess should take him out of the spring and let him sleep upon her bed for three nights. "You," said the prince, "have broken this cruel charm, and now I have nothing to wish for but that you should go with me into my father's kingdom, where I will marry you, and love you as long as you live."

The young princess, you may be sure, was not long in giving her consent; and as they spoke a splendid carriage drove up with eight beautiful horses decked with plumes of feathers and golden harness, and behind rode the prince's servant, the faithful Henry, who had bewailed the misfortune of his dear master so long and bitterly that his heart had well nigh burst. Then all set out full of joy for the prince's kingdom, where they arrived safely, and lived happily a great many years.

Rumpelstiltskin

Germany

Once upon a time there was a miller who was poor, but who had a beautiful daughter. Now it happened that he got into a conversation with the king and said to him: "I have a daughter who knows the art of turning straw into gold."

So the king immediately sent for the miller's daughter and ordered her to turn a whole room full of straw into gold in one night. And if she could not do it, she would have to die. She was locked in the room, and she sat there and cried, because for her life she did not know how the straw would turn into gold.

Then suddenly a little man appeared before her, and said: "What will you give me, if I turn this all into gold?" She took off her necklace and gave it to the little man, and he did what he had promised.

The next morning the king found the room filled with gold, and his heart became even more greedy. He put the miller's daughter into an even larger room filled with straw, and told her to turn it into gold. The little man came again. She gave him a ring from her hand, and he turned it all into gold.

The third night the king had her locked in a third room, which was larger than the first two, and entirely filled with straw. "If you succeed this time, I'll make you my wife," he said.

Then the little man came and said, "I'll do it again, but you must promise me the first child that you have with the king."

In her distress she made the promise, and when the king saw that this straw too had been turned into gold, he took the miller's daughter as his wife.

Soon thereafter the queen delivered a child. Then the little man appeared before her and demanded the child that had been promised him. The queen begged him to let her keep the child, offering him great riches in its place.

Finally he said, "I'll be back to get the child in three days. But if by then you know my name, you can keep the child."

For two days the queen pondered what the little man's name might be, but she could not think of anything, and became very sad. On the third day the king came home from a hunt and told her how, two days earlier, while hunting deep in a dark forest, he had come upon a little house. A comical little man was there, jumping about as if on one leg, and crying out:

Today I'll bake; tomorrow I'll brew.

Then I'll fetch the queen's new child.

It is good that no one knows

Rumpelstiltskin is my name.

The queen was overjoyed to hear this.

Then the dangerous little man arrived and asked: "Your majesty, what is my name?"

"Is your name Conrad?"

"No."

"Is your name Heinrich?"

"No."

"Then could your name be Rumpelstiltskin?"

"The devil told you that!" cried the little man, and in his anger he plunged his right foot so deep into the earth that his whole leg went in; and then in rage he pulled at his left leg so hard with both hands that he tore himself in two.

The Tale of Peter Rabbit

This eBook is for the use of anyone anywhere at no cost and with almost no restrictions whatsoever. You may copy it, give it away or re-use it under the terms of the Project Gutenberg License included with this eBook or online at www.gutenberg.net

Title: The Tale of Peter Rabbit

Author: Beatrix Potter

Release Date: January 30, 2005 [EBook #14838]

Language: English

*** START OF THIS PROJECT GUTENBERG EBOOK THE TALE OF PETER RABBIT ***

Produced by Robert Cicconetti, Ronald Holder and the PG Online

Distributed Proofreading Team (http://www.pgdp.net).

THE TALE OF PETER RABBIT

BY

BEATRIX POTTER

Peter Rabbit

FREDERICK WARNE

FREDERICK WARNE

First published 1902

Frederick Warne & Co., 1902

Printed and bound in Great Britain by William Clowes
Limited, Beccles and London

Once upon a time there were four little Rabbits, and their names were—

Flopsy,

Mopsy,

Cotton-tail,

and Peter.

They lived with their Mother in a sand-bank, underneath the root of a very big fir-tree.

'Now my dears,' said old Mrs. Rabbit one morning, 'you may go into the fields or down the lane, but don't go into Mr. McGregor's garden: your Father had an accident there; he was put in a pie by Mrs. McGregor.'

'Now run along, and don't get into mischief. I am going out.'

Then old Mrs. Rabbit took a basket and her umbrella, and went through the wood to the baker's. She bought a loaf of brown bread and five currant buns.

Flopsy, Mopsy, and Cotton-tail, who were good little bunnies, went down the lane to gather blackberries:

But Peter, who was very naughty, ran straight away to Mr. McGregor's garden, and squeezed under the gate!

First he ate some lettuces and some French beans; and then he ate some radishes;

And then, feeling rather sick, he went to look for some parsley.

But round the end of a cucumber frame, whom should he meet but Mr. McGregor!

Mr. McGregor was on his hands and knees planting out

young cabbages, but he jumped up and ran after Peter, waving a rake and calling out, 'Stop thief!'

Peter was most dreadfully frightened; he rushed all over the garden, for he had forgotten the way back to the gate.

He lost one of his shoes among the cabbages, and the other shoe amongst the potatoes.

After losing them, he ran on four legs and went faster, so that I think he might have got away altogether if he had not unfortunately run into a gooseberry net, and got caught by the large buttons on his jacket. It was a blue jacket with brass buttons, quite new.

Peter gave himself up for lost, and shed big tears; but his sobs were overheard by some friendly sparrows, who flew to him in great excitement, and implored him to exert himself.

Mr. McGregor came up with a sieve, which he intended to pop upon the top of Peter; but Peter wriggled out just in time, leaving his jacket behind him.

And rushed into the tool-shed, and jumped into a can. It would have been a beautiful thing to hide in, if it had not had so much water in it.

Mr. McGregor was quite sure that Peter was somewhere in the tool-shed, perhaps hidden underneath a flower-pot. He began to turn them over carefully, looking under each.

Presently Peter sneezed—'Kertyschoo!' Mr. McGregor was after him in no time.

And tried to put his foot upon Peter, who jumped out of a window, upsetting three plants. The window was too small for Mr. McGregor, and he was tired of running after Peter. He went back to his work.

Peter sat down to rest; he was out of breath and

trembling with fright, and he had not the least idea which way to go. Also he was very damp with sitting in that can.

After a time he began to wander about, going lippity—lippity—not very fast, and looking all round.

He found a door in a wall; but it was locked, and there was no room for a fat little rabbit to squeeze underneath.

An old mouse was running in and out over the stone doorstep, carrying peas and beans to her family in the wood. Peter asked her the way to the gate, but she had such a large pea in her mouth that she could not answer. She only shook her head at him. Peter began to cry.

Then he tried to find his way straight across the garden, but he became more and more puzzled. Presently, he came to a pond where Mr. McGregor filled his water-cans. A white cat was staring at some gold-fish, she sat very, very still, but now and then the tip of her tail twitched as if it were alive. Peter thought it best to go away without speaking to her; he had heard about cats from his cousin, little Benjamin Bunny.

He went back towards the tool-shed, but suddenly, quite close to him, he heard the noise of a hoe—scr-r-ritch, scratch, scratch, scritch. Peter scuttered underneath the bushes. But presently, as nothing happened, he came out, and climbed upon a wheelbarrow and peeped over. The first thing he saw was Mr. McGregor hoeing onions. His back was turned towards Peter, and beyond him was the gate!

Peter got down very quietly off the wheelbarrow; and started running as fast as he could go, along a straight walk behind some black-currant bushes.

Mr. McGregor caught sight of him at the corner, but Peter did not care. He slipped underneath the gate, and was safe at last in the wood outside the garden.

Mr. McGregor hung up the little jacket and the shoes for a scare-crow to frighten the blackbirds.

Peter never stopped running or looked behind him till he got home to the big fir-tree.

He was so tired that he flopped down upon the nice soft sand on the floor of the rabbit-hole and shut his eyes. His mother was busy cooking; she wondered what he had done with his clothes. It was the second little jacket and pair of shoes that Peter had lost in a fortnight!

I am sorry to say that Peter was not very well during the evening.

His mother put him to bed, and made some camomile tea; and she gave a dose of it to Peter!

'One table-spoonful to be taken at bed-time.'

But Flopsy, Mopsy, and Cotton-tail had bread and milk and blackberries for supper.

THE END

End of Project Gutenberg's The Tale of Peter Rabbit, by Beatrix Potter

*** END OF THIS PROJECT GUTENBERG EBOOK THE TALE OF PETER RABBIT ***

Brer Rabbit and the Wonderful Tar Baby

United States

Retold by S.E. Schlosser

Well now, that rascal Brer Fox hated Brer Rabbit on account of he was always cutting capers and bossing everyone around. So Brer Fox decided to capture and kill Brer Rabbit if it was the last thing he ever did! He thought and he thought until he came up with a plan. He would make a tar baby! Brer Fox went and got some tar and he mixed it with some turpentine and he sculpted it into the figure of a cute little baby. Then he stuck a hat on the Tar Baby and sat her in the middle of the road.

Brer Fox hid himself in the bushes near the road and he waited and waited for Brer Rabbit to come along. At long last, he heard someone whistling and chuckling to himself, and he knew that Brer Rabbit was coming up over the hill. As he reached the top, Brer Rabbit spotted the cute little Tar Baby. Brer Rabbit was surprised. He stopped and stared at this strange creature. He had never seen anything like it before!

"Good Morning," said Brer Rabbit, doffing his hat. "Nice weather we're having."

The Tar Baby said nothing. Brer Fox laid low and grinned an evil grin.

Brer Rabbit tried again. "And how are you feeling this fine day?"

The Tar Baby, she said nothing. Brer Fox grinned an evil grin and lay low in the bushes.

Brer Rabbit frowned. This strange creature was not very

polite. It was beginning to make him mad.

"Ahem!" said Brer Rabbit loudly, wondering if the Tar Baby were deaf. "I said 'HOW ARE YOU THIS MORNING?"

The Tar Baby said nothing. Brer Fox curled up into a ball to hide his laugher. His plan was working perfectly!

"Are you deaf or just rude?" demanded Brer Rabbit, losing his temper. "I can't stand folks that are stuck up! You take off that hat and say 'Howdy-do' or I'm going to give you such a lickin'!"

The Tar Baby just sat in the middle of the road looking as cute as a button and saying nothing at all. Brer Fox rolled over and over under the bushes, fit to bust because he didn't dare laugh out loud.

"I'll learn ya!" Brer Rabbit yelled. He took a swing at the cute little Tar Baby and his paw got stuck in the tar.

"Lemme go or I'll hit you again," shouted Brer Rabbit. The Tar Baby, she said nothing.

"Fine! Be that way," said Brer Rabbit, swinging at the Tar Baby with his free paw. Now both his paws were stuck in the tar, and Brer Fox danced with glee behind the bushes.

"I'm gonna kick the stuffin' out of you," Brer Rabbit said and pounced on the Tar Baby with both feet. They sank deep into the Tar Baby. Brer Rabbit was so furious he head-butted the cute little creature until he was completely covered with tar and unable to move.

Brer Fox leapt out of the bushes and strolled over to Brer Rabbit. "Well, well, what have we here?" he asked, grinning an evil grin.

Brer Rabbit gulped. He was stuck fast. He did some fast thinking while Brer Fox rolled about on the road, laughing himself sick over Brer Rabbit's dilemma.

"I've got you this time, Brer Rabbit," said Brer Fox, jumping up and shaking off the dust. "You've sassed me for the very last time. Now I wonder what I should do with you?"

Brer Rabbit's eyes got very large. "Oh please Brer Fox, whatever you do, please don't throw me into the briar patch."

"Maybe I should roast you over a fire and eat you," mused Brer Fox. "No, that's too much trouble. Maybe I'll hang you instead."

"Roast me! Hang me! Do whatever you please," said Brer Rabbit. "Only please, Brer Fox, please don't throw me into the briar patch."

"If I'm going to hang you, I'll need some string," said Brer Fox. "And I don't have any string handy. But the stream's not far away, so maybe I'll drown you instead."

"Drown me! Roast me! Hang me! Do whatever you please," said Brer Rabbit. "Only please, Brer Fox, please don't throw me into the briar patch."

"The briar patch, eh?" said Brer Fox. "What a wonderful idea! You'll be torn into little pieces!"

Grabbing up the tar-covered rabbit, Brer Fox swung him around and around and then flung him head over heels into the briar patch. Brer Rabbit let out such a scream as he fell that all of Brer Fox's fur stood straight up. Brer Rabbit fell into the briar bushes with a crash and a mighty thump. Then there was silence.

Brer Fox cocked one ear toward the briar patch, listening for whimpers of pain. But he heard nothing. Brer Fox cocked the other ear toward the briar patch, listening for Brer Rabbit's death rattle. He heard nothing.

Then Brer Fox heard someone calling his name. He turned

around and looked up the hill. Brer Rabbit was sitting on a log combing the tar out of his fur with a wood chip and looking smug.

"I was bred and born in the briar patch, Brer Fox," he called. "Born and bred in the briar patch."

And Brer Rabbit skipped away as merry as a cricket while Brer Fox ground his teeth in rage and went home.

Fables

The Jay and the Peacock (Aesop)

A Jay venturing into a yard where Peacocks used to walk, found there a number of feathers which had fallen from the Peacocks when they were moulting. He tied them all to his tail and strutted down towards the Peacocks. When he came near them they soon discovered the cheat, and striding up to him pecked at him and plucked away his borrowed plumes. So the Jay could do no better than go back to the other Jays, who had watched his behaviour from a distance; but they were equally annoyed with him, and told him:

"It is not only fine feathers that make fine birds."

The Crow and the Pitcher (Aesop)

A Crow, half-dead with thirst, came upon a Pitcher which had once been full of water; but when the Crow put its beak into the mouth of the Pitcher he found that only very little water was left in it, and that he could not reach far enough down to get at it. He tried, and he tried, but at last had to give up in despair. Then a thought came to him, and he took a pebble and dropped it into the Pitcher. Then he took another pebble and dropped it into the Pitcher. Then he took another pebble and dropped that into the Pitcher. Then he took another pebble and dropped that into the Pitcher. Then he took another pebble and dropped that into the Pitcher. Then he took another pebble and dropped that into the Pitcher. At last, at last, he saw the water mount up near him, and after casting in a few more pebbles he was able to quench his thirst and save his life.

Little by little does the trick.

Tale of the Three Fishes (Panchatantra)

Three fishes named Anagatavidhata, Pratyutpannamati and Yadbhavishya lived in a certain pond, along with many other fishes.

One afternoon, some fishermen were passing by the pond. They investigated the pond, and agreed that the pond was full of fishes. Since they were already returning after catching fishes, and already had a big haul, they decided to come back the next morning.

They discussed, "This pond is full of fishes, and there are many big ones too. We have never caught fishes in this pond. Let us come back tomorrow morning."

The three fishes were swimming on the surface when they heard the fishermen discuss their plans.

The first fish panicked. He immediately assembled all other fishes and told them what they had heard. He said, "Tomorrow morning, the fishermen will arrive to catch us. I do not want to die like this. So, I will leave with my family at the earliest. I advise all of you to follow me. It will not be wise for anybody to stay here any longer!"

The second fish agreed, "I shall follow you, my friend, for what you say is correct. It will be unwise to remain here anymore!"

But the third fish disagreed. He laughed at the two fishes, and said to the fishes assembled, "See how cowardly these two act! This pond belonged to our forefathers, and it is our home now. For so long, no harm has ever come to the fishes of this pond."

He continued, "Just because some fishermen were discussing their plans is no reason for us to panic and leave our home. Those who agree with me, I advise them to stay where we belong and not go to some unknown place."

Thus, the fishes of the ponds got divided into two groups. The group that wanted to stay laughed at the other group. However, within the very evening, the families of the first two fishes started their journey to a different pond through a small outlet. They were followed by many who believed them.

The next morning the fishermen arrived as they had planned, and trapped all the fishes that remained in the pond by casting nets all over the pond.

Not a single fish was spared and the fishermen were overjoyed with the big haul of fishes that they had caught.

The wise indeed say:

When you see a danger coming, act immediately.

The Lion that Sprang to Life (Panchatantra) - OPTIONAL

There lived four friends in a certain town. Although, all four of them were young Brahmins, one of them was a complete ignorant in matters of learning but had good common-sense. The other three were very learned in matters of the Holy Scriptures, but lacked common-sense.

One day, as the four friends were assembled together, they decided, "The scholarship that we have over the Holy Scriptures is no good, if we cannot use it to impress the king, or otherwise to earn money!"

They decided to travel, in order to earn money using their learnings. But the fourth friend was not learned, so they thought of leaving him behind. They agreed, "What good is common-sense? His talents would not help in earning money, let only three of us travel."

After much pleading by the fourth Brahmin, they decide, "It will not be correct to behave like this to a dear friend, Let us take him along with us! We should also share a part of our earnings with him!"

As decided, the four of them started travelling. As they were travelling through a jungle, they noticed the bones of a dead lion, lying on their way. One of them said, "Let us start using our scholarship! We have a dead lion in front of us. Let us test our scholarship, and try to bring life into it!"

While the three Brahmins agreed, the fourth Brahmin did not like the idea. But his preference was ignored by the other three Brahmins, and they started holy rituals.

One of the Brahmins collected the bones of the lion and using his scholarship, created a skeleton of the lion. Another Brahmin used his scholarship to cover the skeleton with flesh and skin. As the lifeless lion stood in front of them, the third Brahmin initiated the rituals to put life into the lion.

The fourth Brahmin was alarmed, "O friends, if the lion comes to life, he will kill all of us! Please stop what you are doing!"

The Brahmins ridiculed him, "After reaching so far, are we going to waste our knowledge? You say so, because you are jealous of our scholarship!"

The fourth Brahmin knew there was no point in arguing with them. He pleaded, "Please give me a moment. I wish to climb a tree before you make use of you scholarship."

He started climbing up a big tree, and could see from above the third Brahmin use his scholarship, to put life into the lion.

As soon as the lion became lively, he noticed the three Brahmins, who were celebrating their successful implementation of their scholarship. The lion immediately pounced on them and killed them.

The fourth Brahmin could do nothing but wait till the lion had gone. Then, he climbed down the tree and returned home alone.

The wise indeed say:

Common sense is preferable to knowledge.

The Frog

Austria

A man and a woman had no children, although they would have given their lives to have some. They prayed for offspring, under any conditions. It appeared that heaven had mercy on them, but when the time came, the newborn was a female frog.

Not letting themselves be distracted, the man and the woman raised her. They taught her music and all kinds of skills.

Above all else the frog loved to sing, and she trained her voice and her range until one would think she was the best singer from the city. Other people had not seen the frog and thought indeed that she was an unknown singer and could not explain why she did not perform in public.

One day the king's son passed by the house and heard the frog singing. He stopped and listened for a long time. He immediately fell in love with the unknown singer and approached her father with a request for permission to see her and speak with her, but the father refused.

The prince heard her sing again and fell even more deeply in love with her. He demanded that her father give her to him in marriage. The father replied that he would have to ask his daughter. The frog agreed under the conditions that she be taken to the royal castle in an enclosed carriage and that she be allowed to enter the bridal chamber without being seen. The prince, his curiosity even more aroused, accepted the conditions.

On the appointed day the frog rode to the royal castle in a tightly enclosed carriage and made her way to the splendid bridal chamber without being seen. She hid herself in one of the two beds that were there. The prince came that evening and was astonished when he could not find his bride. Disappointed, he went to bed.

At midnight the frog crept out of the cushions and onto the prince's breast. Half asleep, he took the frog into his hand and threw her to the floor. She hopped angrily down the steps and home.

The next morning the prince was sorry that he had thrown the frog to the floor, and he became sad and melancholy.

Some time later he went back to the house. Hearing singing, he fell madly in love and began courting his bride anew. The frog accepted, this time without setting any conditions. She made a little carriage out of cardboard, hitched a rooster to it, and drove it herself to the royal castle.

Three fairies were standing in the road. One of them had swallowed a fishbone, which stuck in her throat and was causing her great pain. When the three of them saw the frog driving by in her little carriage and cracking her whip so merrily, they all laughed out with joy. The fishbone dislodged itself from the one fairy's throat, freeing her suddenly of her pain.

They approached the frog, and the first one said, "I will give you a beautiful carriage with horses and servants!" And in an instant a carriage was there with horses and servants in beautiful livery.

Then the second one said, "I will give you expensive clothes and gold and silver!" And in an instant it was all there, gleaming and shimmering, and it was such a joy.

Then came the third fairy, the one who had been freed of the fishbone by laughing, and she said, "I will transform you!"

In that instant the frog became a beautiful maiden. She graciously thanked the three kind fairies and drove happily to the royal castle and to her jubilant and joyful wedding.

The Story of the Devotee Who Spilt the Jar of Honey and Oil

India

They have related that a pious man had a house in the vicinity of a merchant, and lived happily through favor of his neighborly kindness. The merchant continually sold honey and oil, and made his profits by that traffic in unctuous and sweet commodities. Inasmuch as the pious man lived a blameless life, and ever sowed in the field of his guileless heart the seed of the love of God, the merchant reposed implicit confidence in him, and took the supply of his wants upon himself. And in this very thing is the use of riches: to win over the hearts of the poor, and to raise up a perpetual provision from perishable wealth.

The merchant, too, considering the opportunity of doing good a blessing, sent every day somewhat from the stock, in the buying and selling of which he was occupied, for the support of the devotee. The latter used somewhat of this and stored up the rest in a corner. In a short time a jar was filled by these means.

One day the pious man looked into that jar, and thought thus to himself, "Well, now! What quantity of honey and oil is collected in this vessel?"

At last he conjectured ten *mans* to be there, and said:

If I can sell these for ten dirhams, I can buy for that sum five ewes, and these five will each have young every six months, and each will have two lambs. Thus in a year there will be twenty-five, and in ten years from their progeny there will be herds upon herds. So by these means I shall have an abundant supply, and will sell some, and lay in a handsome stock of furniture, and wed a wife of a noble family.

After nine months, I shall have a son born to me, who will study science and polite manners. However, when the weakness of infancy is exchanged for the strength of youth, and that graceful cypress grows up in the garden of manhood, it is probable that he may transgress my orders, and begin to be refractory, and in that case it will be necessary for me to correct him, and I will do so with this very staff which I hold in my hand.

He then lifted up his staff, and was so immersed in thought, that, fancying the head and neck of his rebellious son before him, he brought down the staff, and struck it on the jar of honey and oil. It happened that the jar was placed on a shelf, beneath which he sat with it facing him. As soon as his staff reached the jar, it broke it, and let out the honey and oil all over the head and face and vest and hair of the pious man.

The Mirror of Matsuyama

Japan

In ancient days there lived in a remote part of Japan a man and his wife, and they were blessed with a little girl, who was the pet and idol of her parents. On one occasion the man was called away on business in distant Kyoto. Before he went he told his daughter that if she were good and dutiful to her mother he would bring her back a present she would prize very highly. Then the good man took his departure, mother and daughter watching him go.

At last he returned to his home, and after his wife and child had taken off his large hat and sandals he sat down upon the white mats and opened a bamboo basket, watching the eager gaze of his little child. He took out a wonderful doll and a lacquer box of cakes and put them into her outstretched hands. Once more he dived into his basket, and presented his wife with a metal mirror. Its convex surface shone brightly, while upon its back there was a design of pine trees and storks.

The good man's wife had never seen a mirror before, and on gazing into it she was under the impression that another woman looked out upon her as she gazed with growing wonder. Her husband explained the mystery and bade her take great care of the mirror.

Not long after this happy homecoming and distribution of presents the woman became very ill. Just before she died she called to her little daughter, and said: "Dear child, when I am dead take every care of your father. You will miss me when I have left you. But take this mirror, and when you feel most lonely look into it and you will always see me." Having said these words she passed away.

In due time the man married again, and his wife was not at all kind to her stepdaughter. But the little one, remembering her mother's words, would retire to a corner and eagerly look into the mirror, where it seemed to her that she saw her dear mother's face, not drawn in pain as she had seen it on her deathbed, but young and beautiful.

One day this child's stepmother chanced to see her crouching in a corner over an object she could not quite see, murmuring to herself. This ignorant woman, who detested the child and believed that her stepdaughter detested her in return, fancied that this little one was performing some strange magical art--perhaps making an image and sticking pins into it. Full of these notions, the stepmother went to her husband and told him that his wicked child was doing her best to kill her by witchcraft.

When the master of the house had listened to this extraordinary recital he went straight to his daughter's room. He took her by surprise, and immediately the girl saw him she slipped the mirror into her sleeve. For the first time her doting father grew angry, and he feared that there was, after all, truth in what his wife had told him, and he repeated her tale forthwith.

When his daughter had heard this unjust accusation she was amazed at her father's words, and she told him that she loved him far too well ever to attempt or wish to kill his wife, who she knew was dear to him.

"What have you hidden in your sleeve?" said her father, only half convinced and still much puzzled.

"The mirror you gave my mother, and which she on her deathbed gave to me. Every time I look into its shining surface I see the face of my dear mother, young and beautiful. When my heart aches--and oh! it has ached so much lately--I take out the mirror, and mother's face, with sweet, kind smile, brings me peace, and helps me to

45

bear hard words and cross looks."

Then the man understood and loved his child the more for her filial piety. Even the girl's stepmother, when she knew what had really taken place, was ashamed and asked forgiveness. And this child, who believed she had seen her mother's face in the mirror, forgave, and trouble forever departed from the home.